PROMOTE YOUR BOOK

NAVIGATE THE
WITH MARKETING MAZE
WITH CONFIDENCE

VICTOR KWEGYIR

THE CONFIDENT AUTHOR SERIES:
MASTER THE ART OF WRITING, PUBLISHING, AND STRATEGICALLY
PROMOTING YOUR BOOK FOR SUCCESS

PROMOTE YOUR BOOK
Navigate The Marketing Maze With Confidence

Unless otherwise indicated, all quotes are taken from *Business 365: Daily Inspiration for Creativity, Innovation and Business Success* by Victor Kwegyir[1]

Publisher
Vike Springs Publishing Ltd. www.vikesprings.com

First Edition
ISBN-13: 978-1-918185-02-7- E-book
ISBN-13: 978-1-918185-03-4- Paperback
ISBN-13: 978-1-918185-04-1- Audiobook

Printed in the United Kingdom and United States of America
For bulk orders, book writing, coaching and publishing services, as well as bookings for speaking engagements, contact us: admin@vikesprings.com

LIMIT OF LIABILITY/DISCLAIMER OF WARRANTY

This publication is designed to provide accurate and authoritative information in regard to the subject matter covered. It is sold with the understanding that the publisher and author make no representations or warranties with respect to the completeness of the contents of this work. Neither the publisher nor the author shall be liable for any damages or losses arising herefrom. The fact that an organisation or website is referred to in this work as a citation and/or a potential source of further information does not mean that the author or the publisher endorses the information that the organisation or website may provide, or recommendations it may make. Due to the ever-changing information from the web, internet websites and URLs listed in this work may have changed or been removed. All trademarks or names referenced in this book are the property of their respective owners, and the publisher and author are not associated with any product or vendor mentioned.

DEDICATION

To our authors: we always appreciate
you for choosing us.

Keep pouring out your heart, thoughts, expertise
and wisdom, and we will continue to help you realise
all your publication aims, one book at a time.

Your success is our greatest motivation!

CONTENTS

INTRODUCTION

The publishing industry is evolving and growing each day. Not only is there an ongoing increase in the number of books, but there is also a widening variety of the many formats and platforms where books can be accessed and read. Each day more people are considering penning their thoughts and ideas to share with the world, and almost everyone has the belief that their book can be a bestseller. It's an uncomfortable truth that not many books make bestseller lists, although there are many bestseller-promoting schemes that don't reflect actual sales. Having a book that sells well and reaches a wide audience has a direct correlation with how the book is promoted.

Whether you are a new author looking to launch a debut publication, or an established writer who is looking to boost visibility in this competitive market, when it comes to marketing you will find there are many options to choose from. These include traditional ways to market your book, and also some innovative and creative ways to boost sales.

In this book I will address all the essential components that need to be in place in order to get your book strategically positioned for marketing. There is also a lot you can do yourself with your own connections and abilities, and you will be able to understand more about this aspect of promoting your book and becoming a successful author.

Understanding your audience is key to choosing your marketing strategy and this will depend on your book's unique selling point (USP). Knowing what stands out about your particular publication will lead you to recognise the readership you will target to boost sales.

It's not just about your book – it's about your brand, your unique identity as an author. By developing an online presence that connects with your readership, you are able to generate interest in your life and your book, and this will develop into other avenues that will connect and generate income. Your online presence is delivered through many platforms, and understanding your audience will lead you to the most effective ways to establish yourself.

Book marketers offer marketing schemes that will help your book become visible in the literary world. Publicising your book helps to promote your profile, with the potential to attain popularity on a global scale. When you begin to recognise and value the importance of a good marketing plan, you will understand the necessity of investing in this aspect of getting your book, your brand and your sphere of influence into the public arena. Please realise that it is not just about writing a good book, and getting the print process done well – it is also about how you raise awareness about your writing and who you are.

Book signings, media appearances, press coverage and paid advertising can also be part of your marketing plan, and you will be able to identify a wealth of possibilities through online sales channels.

It is also good practice to use ways to measure your success so that you can target your efforts more effectively. Evaluation and feedback need to be part of your marketing strategy.

Vike Springs Publishing or other publishers can guide you when you are developing your sales plan, and can offer ways to market through their own routes and contacts with specially designed branding, marketing and promotion. However, it is good to be aware of the many other ways you can sell, and information in this book will open up further areas for you to explore.

This is the third book in *The Confident Author Series: Master the Art of Writing, Publishing and Strategically Promoting your Book for Success*. These books are not meant to be digested in a linear fashion – even when starting your writing journey, you will need to be aware of the next steps, and in particular your marketing strategy should be in place very early on. Marketing your book begins from the day the book idea is conceived. Waiting until the book is published to start thinking about how you will sell is nearly always too late.

Throughout these books you will find quotes to encourage and motivate on this mission to 'transform the world globally through words'.

"If it is worth the time, it is worth giving it your all."

CHAPTER 1

SOME FACTS AND FIGURES ABOUT THE PUBLISHING INDUSTRY

Projecting for the next five years, global book sales should reach $82.7 billion in 2027, with an average annual growth of 1.48%.[2]

Print books are generating over $64.35 billion in revenue as of 2023. This will be a 2.24% increase over 2022.[3]

Self-publishing gives authors more control over the publishing process. With about 1.7 million titles self-published, this route underscores a significant shift in how books reach readers. The self-publishing model allows authors to bypass traditional gatekeepers, offering a direct path to market through platforms like Amazon's Kindle Direct Publishing, Smashwords, and Lulu.[4]

eBooks have been growing globally by 3.52% annually since 2017 on average, and were projected to generate over $13.72 billion in 2023. This book format is projected to grow faster than print books, and the revenue should reach $15.29 billion in 2027.[5]

Audiobooks contributed to 5.73% of all book sales worldwide in 2021, and in 2027, audiobooks are projected to account for over 6.9% of global book sales, increasing the share by 27% over 7 years.[6]

The global online book services market is expected to grow at a compound annual growth rate (CAGR) of 5.8% between 2020 and 2027. Market size is expected to expand from $18.8 billion in 2020 to $27.8 billion in 2027.[7]

"Written Word Media's annual survey of more than 2000 authors has consistently shown that successful indie authors use professional cover designers and editors, and also that they write a lot of books. In December 2023 their survey showed that the median number of books was 8 ('median' removes outliers such as those with 300+ books and gives the number an author is most likely to have). It also asked questions around direct book sales, with a growing but still minority of authors engaging in direct sales and the tools they most frequently used to do so."[8]

Publishing frequency and genre diversity: many self-published creators are prolific, with over half publishing more than 10 books. Romance, fantasy, and crime/thriller genres dominate, accounting for 57% of self-published books.[9]

"Focus on doing what you love, do it well and you will achieve success."

CHAPTER 2

WHAT IS MARKETING?

Definition: The activity or business of promoting and selling products or services, including market research and advertising.

The four basic marketing principles of Product, Price, Place, and Promotion are interconnected and are known as Marketing Mix.

There are three phases of a strategic marketing process:

- Planning
- Implementation
- Evaluation.

The 'Marketing Rule of 7' states that a prospect needs to 'hear' the advertiser's message at least seven times before they'll take action to buy that product or service.

The 7-11-4 rule in marketing suggests that a buyer needs seven hours of interaction, across eleven touch points, in four separate locations before they make a purchase.

> *"Keep your eyes on the ball if the object of being in the game is to score goals."*

WHAT IS BOOK MARKETING?

Book marketing is the process of converting potential readers into people who buy your books.

The goal of book marketing is to generate awareness of the book to attract the attention of readers and sellers through avenues such as advertising, industry reviews, newsletters, author websites, social media pages, personal engagement, and more.

Your book is a product. Marketing is how you sell that product. Just telling people about your book isn't enough to get sales; you need to sell the value it adds and benefits that will be experienced by your purchasers.

So many budding authors believe that a good book will sell itself. Unfortunately, that is not the case, and as much thought and energy needs to go into a marketing plan as the effort and dedication needed to write. It's important to get it right – from building anticipation to the often-unrecognised world of metadata. Every book you sell should lead to increasing interest, buyer recommendations and ongoing sales, and a strategic plan will aid that process.

> *"Successful people don't just work hard, they work smart. And that, my friend, is the basis of strategy!"*

SALES DON'T JUST HAPPEN!

Many authors believe that once they have written 'The End' on their manuscript that their job is finished. They get a shock when they realise that it's just the start, and there is editing, design, proofreading, formatting, printing and distribution to be done, and that these elements are just as crucial to the success of the book.

You may have produced the most amazing book, but how will readers know that your book exists if it doesn't appear on the literary radar? This is why correctly marketing your book is so important.

Having a good marketing strategy is vital to the success or failure of your book, and these days authors need to be fully engaged with their book promotion, instead of relying on their publisher.

Many authors fail to understand that the publishing process is interlinked, and each stage impacts the final goal. To get the best results you must give attention to each stage in the process and ensure it is delivered professionally.

Although the self-publishing market is booming, did you know that 90% of self-published books sell less than 100 copies and 20% of authors report no income? Another statistic says that among authors who published their first book in the last 10 years, earnings over $25,000 per year have been reported by more self-published authors than those who went down the traditional publishing route.[10] That is a big difference, and goes to show that if you want your book to sell, you have to pay attention to how you are going to get sales. The road to becoming an actual bestseller is directly linked to how you market your book. I write this from experience, as I have sold thousands of copies of my own books, and helped many other authors do the same.

> *Purpose is too powerful and addictive*
> *to let you go once you find it.*

BECOME A GOOD BUSINESS ENTREPRENEUR

Publishing a book, or series of books, is not just about the literary side of things. There is also the business aspect. The average author isn't necessarily a business person, so there is a need to understand and embrace the business side of book publishing, which centres around marketing the book. Publishing has to be viewed as an investment that carries the potential of significant returns. This changes the game altogether.

An important point to note as an author is that everything about your publication is associated with you, irrespective of the genre of the book. This means that just as a good book raises your value or level of authority on a subject, it is affected negatively if the quality is compromised.

Writing and publishing a book is one of the smartest ways to establish your brand. With that in mind it makes sense that to do this well requires investing in excellent professional services and processes, in order to produce a book that a potential reader would be happy to buy. Even more importantly, your readers can become loyal fans, who will go on to tell others about your work and be keen to purchase your next book, sign up for your seminar, spend time and resources to come and listen to your talk, subscribe to your show, or even sign up for a coaching service, or any of the opportunities publishing offers you beyond the selling of books.

If publishing a book is like building a brand it is important to go through the process professionally and systematically to get it right at each stage in order to earn the respect and trust of the readers and ensure that the quality of your book registers in the mind of readers and potential readers. You demonstrate that 'I know what I am doing', and that you are committed to giving them the best experience and value for money when they invest in you and your work.

WRITE MORE BOOKS

Writing more sells more! This should be the mantra of every aspiring author, as it is an important marketing strategy which is often overlooked.

Simply put, your net earnings from sales will depend on how much you have spent on publication and marketing, and also the fees from the platform you are selling from. This means that the more you sell, the more profit you will make. With statistics showing 90% of self-published books sell less than 100 copies, there will be a lot of pressure on that one book to sell enough copies for you to realise a profit.

The most profitable authors are those who have published several books, and this applies to both fiction and non-fiction. The more books you have published, the more chance of a sale, and the more chance that someone who buys one of your books will buy another – or even all of your books. Ultimately you get the opportunity to build your own tribe of readers and followers.

In Chapter 5, I write about the advantages and disadvantages of exclusivity. Authors who have many books are able to spread their books over various platforms, taking advantage of the benefits of exclusivity for a particular book whilst also selling other books on the wide range of platforms.

> *"If your mindset is wrong, very little will go right.*
> *If it is right, then it is gold. Because you will*
> *eventually get to where you want to be."*

CHAPTER **3**

MARKETING STRATEGY

The possibilities are endless, and can be as creative as you like – as long as what you do brings a return in increased sales. Research ways in which people are promoting their books, particularly in your genre, to see if there are interesting paths you wish to pursue.

Good book marketing builds an attractive author brand, and this leads to a healthy author platform capable of converting a one-time buyer into a fan for life. Rather than being 'salesy' your book marketing should help foster relationships, with both readers and booksellers.

Your author platform will involve many different aspects, but the main aim about developing your author platform is to reach your customers and get them to the point of purchase. Your platform will be found on social media, email lists, blogs and podcasts, interviews, book signings, and more. Another great opportunity is found in your book itself, whether through the author bio, or in the end matter of your book, where you can tempt the reader towards buying another of your books, or encourage them to become more involved in your journey.

Writing more books helps your visibility. It's a very popular strategy – once a reader has purchased one of your books, they are more likely to choose something else you have written than take a risk on an unfamiliar author.

In *Get Writing*, you learnt how important it is to determine who you are writing for. When considering your marketing and promotion, you also need to determine where your readers are. Are they on a certain aspect of social media, or do they buy certain magazines, or attend certain events? Knowing more about where to find your readership helps you when building an author platform. It provides a bridge so that your target audience can easily find you, become aware of other books you have written, and eagerly await release of your next published work.

Remember that selling a book is different to selling other products that are necessities. Buyers need to be convinced that a book purchase will address a need that they have – whether it is for relaxation (a summer read), education, or transformation. When you identify what need your book will address, you will be in a better position to target your readership effectively.

30 WAYS TO OPTIMISE YOUR MARKETING STRATEGY

Consider these options when planning your marketing strategy. Depending on the genre of your book, you will find that some of these options are a natural fit and can be done easily. Other ideas may take more ingenuity, but all these areas are worth time and effort as you discover which routes lead to sales.

Keep a check list of what you are doing, and break your goals down into weekly, monthly or annual tasks. Your strategy can be adapted so you can drop areas that don't work well, and include new areas you want to develop. However, don't give up too soon. It's important to be consistent and build exposure in whatever area you choose to pursue. Many authors give up on promotional ideas too early, so before you give up on, say, an ad on social media, or speaking engagements, make sure you stick with it until you begin to get some results, or until it is very clear that it isn't working. You should also keep an eye on any new marketing ideas that emerge and don't be afraid to try something different from time to time.

BEFORE AND WHILE WRITING

1. **Consider who can promote you.** The **Foreword** in your book can significantly boost sales. Look at your network and consider reaching out to mentors, experts, academics, or anyone with authority or a strong connection to your subject. A good Foreword lends credibility and helps attract a wider audience, as buyers are more likely to show interest when they see a respected name endorsing your work. If you have a number of endorsements from well-known individuals who've read advance copies, you can feature their recommendations on a separate endorsements page or as brief quotes on the cover. The **Acknowledgements** section can also support your book's success. It's an opportunity to express genuine thanks to those who have supported you throughout your journey. Recognising their contributions honours their involvement and can also lead to them becoming ambassadors for your work, as they promote your book within their own circles, creating more visibility.

2. **Clearly identify your target audience and where it can be found.** Look at how your prospective readership reviews books in the same genre – note what they value and what they don't like. Make sure that your writing addresses what they are looking for.

3. **Join forums and groups.** Before and during writing, join forums and groups relevant to your subject and engage on a consistent basis. This will set you up to be noticed. You will gain a reputation as an expert or authority, or just someone who is passionate about your subject, and it helps you to build a following.

4. **Connect with potential readers.** Write and share articles on the subject of your book on all relevant available platforms. For example, a simple website or blog is where you can begin to connect with people who will be interested in your genre of books, and where you can invite them to subscribe to regular emails from you. Building up a list of contacts in this way is very effective, as these people can become engaged in your writing process, get links to other information, and be informed of special offers or giveaways. The more exposure they have to your book or books, the more likely it is that they will make a purchase. Don't overdo the emails, but keep them interesting – help the people who receive them to feel invested in you and your journey. And ensure the communications are well-written and error-free. In all your communication, be very clear as to what you want as a response, whether it's a pre-order, a review, or a comment about what you have shared with them. Help your readers to help you!

5. **Build anticipation.** Keep updating your pages as you build anticipation. You can even include excerpts from your book once it approaches completion, and encourage feedback that will help you to target your readership accurately, ensuring you are producing what they want to read. You can also offer discounts on pre-orders of your book. Even if you haven't published yet, you can start a countdown to release day, and give details about book signings or appearances.

6. **Promote your identity.** Look to publicise yourself using keywords or taglines, so you will be instantly recognisable.

7. **Make time.** Budget your time and resources for developing a marketing plan and strategy.

8. **Research the best time to launch.** Do some research on the best time of year to publish your book to maximise sales. For example, if the book is likely to be an attractive gift option, ensure you launch in good time before the Christmas market gets underway – consider publishing in October so that your book can be marketed and promoted before the peak holiday season. Timing is also significant for books that are of interest for the academic year, or for summer reads.

DURING PUBLISHING

9. **Create awareness, anticipation and excitement**. Use WATCH THIS SPACE, COMING SOON and NEW RELEASE posters on all your social media pages and network platforms, including showing them as your profile photo. These often get your network talking and asking questions and is an opportunity to generate the anticipation you need before the launch and release of the book.

10. **Use all publishing formats.** Depending on your budget, make sure your book is accessible in all formats – eBook, paperback, hardback and audiobook (Vike Springs Publishing packages offer all options). You may need to balance projected sales with budget, but certainly consider print-on-demand options for paperback and hardback if you anticipate your sales in those areas are difficult to quantify. In order to maximise your influence, you need to publish in as many formats as you can, and an eBook version is a must, as many people find it easier to buy with a click and a download rather than incurring the extra cost of a print book and associated costs of delivery.

11. **Use all distribution platforms.** Make the book available on all platforms (see Chapter 6 for detailed information about this). Vike Springs Publishing ensures all books are made available and distributed

to all global bookseller platforms worldwide, as well as through its global retail partners.

12. **Pursue all existing contacts.** Your friends, family, colleagues and existing network are a cost-effective way to find an audience for your writing. Ask for their help and make it easy for them to help you. Reward every new fan as if they were your only fan.

13. **Contact organisations and bodies related to the subject of your book**. Offer to appear as a guest speaker, offer sample copies of your book, donate to specific organisations if you think it will offer you greater visibility to generate potential sales and opportunities at some point in the future.

14. **Use all social media platforms** – Facebook, Instagram, X/Twitter, WhatsApp, LinkedIn, TikTok with videos. Use good quality posts and compelling write-up to generate excitement. Be regular in your input so that users will recognise you as a presence. You need to build a reputation, so be consistent.

15. **Participate in social networks for authors**. Engage in discussions and become a presence. For example, Wattpad is a forum for fiction writers, and Bookbub allows posts from new authors promoting their books.

16. **Target influencers with huge followings**. Influencers need a constant stream of material so this is a rich source of potential publicity. Search for social media influencers who promote books in your genre, who have a huge follower base, and have high responses to their posts. Contact them directly with special offers or other aspects that will tap into their own promotional direction. Once you have established a relationship with an influencer, or influencers, there's the potential for future publicity as well, and they can be approached for commendations, as listed in point 1.

17. **Continue to blog** and make contact with bloggers who blog on your subject, sharing information about your book so they can write about it.

18. **Release a podcast**, host someone linked to your book on it, or become a guest on someone else's podcast.

19. **Plan and work towards a book launch** – see a range of ideas below about launching your book. This is one of the smartest ways to give your new book a major boost of exposure to everyone around you 'without an apology.'

20. **Contact local bookstores and libraries**, pushing the local author interest angle.

21. **Contact non-traditional stores** including flea markets and pop-up shops at events.

22. **Use ads.** Consider using Amazon ads, and ads on social media platforms, even ads on the radio. Don't be shy – believe in your product and convince others that it's the best. Be aware that advertising on-line through social media platforms has a distinct aspect, (except in cases where you may have already built your audience around the subject of your book). The people you will engage with may not necessarily be looking for a book to buy. You need to engage them, so they enter your sphere of influence, to find out more about you and your message, in order to entice them into buying your book.

23. **HARO.** This stands for Help a Reporter Out and is an online platform that connects journalists and bloggers with experts on particular subjects. When your response to a query is accepted, it brings increased online visibility and connects to a wider audience. This was one of the platforms I tapped into when I published my first book, giving me an opportunity to be a radio and TV guest on over 80 shows across UK, USA, Canada and other online media platforms.

24. **Media personalities and influencers.** Connect with media personalities and influencers by sending a onesheet, which is a summary of you and your project. This can be your blurb, or author bio. Engaging with a media personality will widen awareness and draw more readers towards you. It is important to do your research here to ensure that the particular platform, radio, TV or podcast will align with your targeted readership.

25. **Get on lists!** Getting on any list, whether it is about your subject, or as an interesting new publication, will draw attention to you and boost sales.

26. **Join book reading groups.** Consider using Goodreads, an online book reading website, contact book clubs whether local groups or online groups, offer price promotions, even donate a book as a raffle prize – don't hold back but get your name and your book into public view.

27. **Check your visibility.** Keep reviewing your presence online – when people type in your name or the name of your book, what do they see? Check your SEO (Search Engine Optimisation) and if you are struggling to make this work for you, consider getting the advice of someone with the right technical knowledge to help you.

28. **Use AI to help readers find you**. You have probably noticed that using a search engine nowadays directs you to an AI overview instead of a list of websites. How this works for directing people to your book is different from focusing on key words and meta data. This is a more in-depth approach that seeks to understand user preferences and looks at GEO rather than SEO. GEO stands for Generative Engine Optimisation, and the AI platform will identify sources of information that will give broader parameters to search results and seek to tailor them to what it thinks you want (which may be different to another user). To make the most of AI search results, use all of our recommendations to publish and publicise across all mediums, make sure your content is set out well so that AI can understand it, and do your own research, using different AI models to understand the range of results that can be achieved.

29. **Use QR codes.** A QR code is a fairly recent tool used by authors and publishers to enhance reader experience. Although often only noticed on the book's cover, QR codes can also be used in the text of the book to direct readers to more information, such as videos and other more detailed information that has not been included in the book itself. QR codes can also be used on all author promotional material to direct users to areas that are of interest, such as book signings,

new publications, reviews, etc. You can even use a QR code to allow a reader to listen to an excerpt from your book in audio format. When used in the right way, QR codes build connections between reader and author. Your logo can also be shown in your QR code to provide instant recognition of your brand.

30. **Use AI to make promotional material!** You can use AI to summarise your book and from there to develop ads, videos, and other teasers to get your readers on board. So whether you are blogging, putting material on a website, promoting through social media, or raising your profile by other means, the development of AI offers a wealth of opportunity.

Book Marketing Strategy

- Friends, Family, Fan base
- Social Media Platforms
- Blogs/website/podcast
- Ads Amazon & Other
- Local Groups/Libraries
- Forums
- Book launch

"Although it can be excruciating, challenges are promotional stepping stones to the next level."

MAKE A BOOK LAUNCH MEMORABLE

There is no limit to how creative you can be with a book launch, and this can be a virtual launch, or one that is in a physical space.

First consider what aspects of your book can be linked to other events, and follow that through to joining in with already established activities. (See No 8 in the 30 Steps above about targeting your sales strategy to align with significant events.) Alternatively, if you have connected with groups that share your interest, you can opt to present and launch your book to them. The more real you can make the event, the more your audience will be enticed to walk away with one of your books. Think about small giveaways that will identify you and your book, or maybe act out or demonstrate a particular section that is in your book.

To stimulate your creativity, here are some ideas:

- A book about cookery – a cookery demonstration is performed in a shopping area.
- A mystery thriller – the author joins a mystery weekend as one of her characters.
- A sci-fi book – membership cards to a secret organisation are given to passers-by.
- The book is linked to a charity connection – the launch takes place to raise funds for the charity. (For example, this could be a book about animals, or social justice.)
- The formal hire of a venue, where the author invites other new writers to present their books, as well as his own.
- An online podcast, or live event on social media, inviting audience participation.

Whatever your choice (and budget), make sure you direct people to how to buy your book. Make sure they understand how it will enhance their lives, and let them know how they can inform others of your new product.

"No one becomes better at something by partial commitment. You are either all in or all out."

A NOTE ABOUT DIRECT-TO-CONSUMER (D2C) SALES

Many of the marketing options listed above involve D2C sales, which is becoming a popular trend in self-publishing. This sales outlet leads to establishing a personal connection with readers, building a trust relationship with you and your brand. It leaves you free to introduce special offers, generate interest in new projects, and obtain feedback and direction by analysing which of your marketing tools are getting the most traffic, or what actions are actually generating sales.

The downside of this way of selling is that it can involve a lot of hard work!

"Ideas rule the world. Not debates and arguments."

CHAPTER 4

WORLDWIDE DISTRIBUTION

Your time and money spent on marketing needs to be aligned with getting your book on the right platform, as it doesn't make sense to promote a book if your target audience can't easily access it. Books that are available worldwide can tap into a whole new pool of potential readers and buyers, so no matter where you are based, you will probably want to have an international appeal, and it is important to understand the difference between worldwide publishing and publishing in the UK, or within your particular country of residence. If you opt for worldwide publishing (which is where Vike Springs Publishing is uniquely placed for all our authors), you'll obtain global rights, so you have the authority to sell your book in different countries and manage the publishing rights in those countries.

You will have to target a wider, international and diverse audience, and adapt your promotional efforts for different cultural contexts and consumer behaviour.

Worldwide distribution must also comply with the legal and regulatory requirements of different countries, which includes intellectual property, censorship and distribution rules.

Distribution can involve more complexities, depending on the number of countries involved and the shipping and warehousing needed.

The worldwide aspect of publishing is worth pursuing: in emerging markets, per capita spending on books is forecast to rise due to rising income levels, education, literacy and the increasing availability of less expensive digital publications.[11]

New opportunities such as Asia-Pacific, Latin America and Africa need educational resources, children's literature and local literature. Authors can tap into these resources by offering digital and multilingual content, together with localised marketing strategies.[12]

When considering worldwide distribution, you need to use a publisher with a professional and knowledgeable worldwide perspective. Often authors will not take into consideration book size and other specifications that need to be aligned with international standards; or they choose a publisher with no presence on all the global bookseller platforms, or in all the major formats. There are also times where an author may be a resident in a country with limited accessibility to global bookseller platforms.

Vike Springs Publishing has all the necessary experience to help you navigate the entire publishing process worldwide, including publishing your book in all the four major book formats and making it available worldwide on all the major global bookseller platforms.

The International Publishing Association (IPA)[13] provides up to date information for 76 member countries, covering publishers, ISBN registrations, demographics and literacy, mobile and internet connectivity, information about education systems, a country's policy on books and publishing, and information about local tax issues. The information provided by the IPA helps authors and their publishers to target emerging markets and is invaluable information when planning marketing strategy.

The Alliance of Independent Authors (ALLi) is a global membership organisation for self-published authors and provides data about writing trends and also shows how authors are effectively marketing their books.

"What you make time for says a lot, if not everything, about where you are going in life."

CHAPTER 5

BEHIND THE SCENES

METADATA

Along with ISBNs, metadata is a way of categorising your book so that it can be easily found through search engines, bookstores and libraries. If you want to sell successfully, you will need to incorporate as much appropriate metadata as possible into your publishing strategy. The information you include will depend on the genre and your target audience.

Metadata includes title, author, subtitle, language, price, and ISBN. You should include specific information about genre, location details if that is a feature of your book, and timeframe (e.g. a specific historical period, or a particular year that your publication relates to). Any notable recommendations or accolades can be noted, as well as any big names or organisations that are associated in any way with your book.

Ensure that your metadata is consistent across all your selling platforms.

Metadata, including keywords, can be reviewed, updated and adjusted as you go along, using analytics and sales data to check on performance.

CHOOSING KEYWORDS

Think of your core themes, and identify any words or phrases people might type into a search for a book like yours. Enter them in a book search such as Amazon, and check that your search is bringing up similar titles. A keyword planner, such as one offered by Google, will show how popular these key words are, and also identify words that describe your book but are less competitive, i.e. make it more likely that your book will be identified in a search.

You should end up with a list of not more than 10 keywords, listing the most important first. Now, using your book title together with your list of keywords, draft a book description or blurb, which should be compelling and keyword rich. Do this also with your author bio.

Some platforms allow additional keywords that are not discoverable by readers but help with searches.

Remember that better keywords lead to more sales, and more sales lead to the selling platform, such as

Amazon, placing your book higher up the search list – they promote your book for you.

SALES ALGORITHMS

The number of books sold within the first 30 days is important to booksellers, whose algorithms are set to take notice. However, how these sales are spread out and where they come from are also important. If they result over a few days, rather than concentrated in one day, and if they come from a wider search than someone entering the title of your book, then they carry more weight, as this demonstrates that your metadata is accurate, and your book is attractive to a variety of readers, not just your mother!

Pre-order sales are also very important to these algorithms, as it helps to determine how popular the book will be, and can also project actual sales.

Online booksellers look at the source of traffic. **Direct traffic** is where someone goes directly to your book to purchase it; **social** is where the book is listed in social media and a customer has clicked on it to go to the bookseller site; **paid** is where a customer has clicked on an online ad; a **referral** is where there has been a review on another site and referred through; and finally, **organic**.

An **organic** source of traffic is when a customer has bought your book after browsing through the site. It indicates to the retailer that your book is a solid purchase, and it therefore attracts more search results and more sales velocity.

How your book performs depends on three things initially: accurate metadata so people can find what they want, an attractive price, and whether the book description and cover is compelling enough to make that purchase. After those initial sales, reviews start to also become important in the selling mix.

TAKE NOTE

KDP stands for Kindle Direct Publishing and it is one of the platforms used to self-publish both eBooks and hard copy books. You may find that your KDP account is suspended if you have misrepresented your data, so make sure you get this aspect of your marketing strategy correct by observing the following:

- The title and subtitle must exactly match what is on your book cover. And use the same author name consistently in all books you author.
- Don't overuse keywords.
- Avoid using promotional language such as 'bestselling' or 'free'.
- Accurately describe your book content in your keywords.
- Make sure you place your book in the correct categories and that your metadata information is in line with the genres where you are placing your book.
- It should be a given, but be truthful, don't include

personal information, and make sure you have permission for any images or other information that you use.

If you comply with the above, and ensure you regularly review Amazon's KDP metadata guidelines, you can be confident that you have positioned your book to sell effectively.

> *"Innovation starts with seeing change as an opportunity, not a threat."*

UNDERSTAND THE PROS AND CONS OF EXCLUSIVITY

Exclusivity is the term used where authors decide to sell and promote their book through one outlet only. The advantages include free promotion of your book to a wide audience, the ability to offer promotional discounts, and other areas that promote exposure. This can quickly boost income. It also makes life simpler in trying to track sales and monitor how much interest your book is generating.

The downside of an exclusive arrangement is that your sales will only be made to those who use that particular selling platform, and the terms of your deal with the seller may change. You may discover that the terms of the arrangement are restrictive, or the way the algorithms work 'miss' where your book would have the best selling advantage by placing it alongside other books that don't lead the purchaser to click on your book.

Going Wide is the term used where you engage with different retailers. This can be a good long-term strategy and reach a wider audience, particularly if you want to attract global attention. It can take more time in monitoring and managing sales, but you can get help from your publisher to understand all your options and decide on the best strategy that fits your marketing plan. Vike Springs has mastered this and ensures our authors' books are available worldwide on all the major existing global bookseller platforms and any new ones that come up. We also ensure the right setup and efficient management of each author's book, including royalty payments to authors.

REVIEWS

Reviews from readers have to match the metadata you have supplied. What you want is someone to say your book has exceeded their expectations, not disappointed them.

Good reviews will push organic customers who are viewing search results into actually making that purchase. A large quantity of good reviews will also feed into algorithms and push your book higher up the search engine.

Reviews are also a great source of feedback for authors, who can analyse their marketing approach, the pricing of their book, the title, the cover; and also help them assess if there is a market for a series of books.

Good reviews can be fed back into websites and blogs, which in itself will lead to more sales.

Expect some negative feedback from your readers. Not everyone will be positive. Use constructive criticism to learn to be better, make sure you don't engage in arguments or disputes with people, and choose to focus on the positive feedback you get.

Book reviews validate you, and make you visible to a wider audience. They can give you as a writer, and your sales, a great boost in confidence and prosperity.

> *"The size of your goal counts. Smaller goals can cause you to give up at the most insignificant hurdle. Dream BIG!"*

CHAPTER 6

DISTRIBUTION PLATFORMS

A book distributor is different from a book wholesaler, in that they don't just store and ship your book to bookstores or libraries, but will provide customer service, sales, marketing, warehousing, and shipping. Many publishers, whether trad or hybrid, will also act as distributors for your publication, whether it is a paperback, a hardback, an eBook or in an audio format.

Alternatively, you can find book distributors that specialise in different genres, such as text books, children's books, religious publications and more. Also popular among writers who wish to self-publish are IngramSpark, Amazon KDP, or Lulu. These enable authors to print and distribute paperbacks and hardbacks, and also eBooks.

For digital books, explore Google Play Books, Apple Books, Kobo Writing Life, or Smashwords/Draft2digital.

For audiobooks, distribute through Audible, Amazon, and iTunes via ACX; Findaway Voices run by Spotify distributes to Audible, Google Play, and Libraries. You can also consider Audiobooks.com, OverDrive, Author Republic, Kobo and many more.

Check out the terms and conditions of each of these distributors and listen to the advice of your publisher, or speak to the team at Vike Springs to understand which is the best route for you or how they can help you with your specific requirements.

> *"Don't get bogged down in the end result. It is the process that has all the secrets you need to learn from."*

BESTSELLER LISTS

Different selling platforms have different requirements for a book to achieve bestselling status, and these can be complex.

Bestseller recognition can depend on where your book 'fits' into the genre and how many similar books there are that you are effectively competing with. It will also be dependent on how many sales you achieve within different time frames. Pre-order sales can give a useful boost, as can ARCs (Advance Reader Copies) that generate reviews. Your marketing strategy should take into account the timing of the release of your book and the number of sales you want to generate if you are aiming to achieve bestseller status.

Do your research well in advance about how to get your book noticed in this way, and consult a professional publicist if you think it is something you want to aim for.

Some publishers also offer a Best Seller Programme in-house, and achieving this status will help with your sales.

"Entrepreneurs who pay for expert advice do so because they are smart enough to know ROI (return on investment) is guaranteed."

CHAPTER 7

TRANSLATION SERVICES

On occasions it may be beneficial to have your book translated into another language. Your publisher can arrange for this to be done, and will work with you and the translator to define who has the translation rights and how royalties will be shared, through a formal contract.

The translation should accurately reflect the meaning, tone and style of your book, but adapt cultural differences and colloquial references, so that it can be a quality production that resonates with the new audience.

Editors, proofreaders and beta readers will need to be fluent in the new language, and print layout should be adjusted appropriately, particularly if the language is very different typographically to the English language.

"The greatest barrier to your progression and success in life is the way you think."

CHAPTER 8

FINAL WORDS

By now you will have realised how much is involved in producing and selling a book. Key points to remember:

- Some books take a long time after publishing to actually achieve recognition and become bestsellers, so persevere!
- There are all sorts of possibilities for you when you publish your book – it might lead to making a film, a lecture tour, being consulted as an expert on radio or TV, or more. Keep an open mind and look out for all the different avenues that may develop.

Effective book marketing will increase your book's visibility and increase your sales. The knowledge you have gained through reading this book will enable you to transform your marketing efforts and achieve your publishing goals. Be consistent and keep at it! Track your progress and adapt as you go along. In addition, make sure you avail yourself of the information in my other two books in this three-book series that cover writing and the publishing process so you'll be confident in all aspects of book authorship and publication.

If all that I have shared here seems daunting or complicated, please remember that the Vike Springs team is at hand to help with any queries you may have. We provide a range of services that covers the entire spectrum of the book writing, publishing and marketing process.

Vike Springs Publishing aims to ensure that your book publishing experience matches your expectations, and we provide a wide range of options with our comprehensive publishing services, together with quality printing and worldwide distribution. By assessing your manuscript on sign-up, our team can immediately propose the marketing strategies that will work best for you. We offer a professional perspective, but give you the freedom of choice to make the final decision in how you wish to proceed.

Vike Springs is the publisher, distributer and printer of choice for authors worldwide, including those based in Africa, who wish to have global exposure and readership. We have published for clients from almost every continent to date. We ensure that each title meets international press editorial standards so you can have complete confidence in our expertise.

We are here for you on every step of your journey. Don't hesitate to contact us for any query you may have. A full list of our services is shown in Appendix 1.

> *"A good book today will be a*
> *good book ten years from today,*
> *but it has to be promoted*
> *properly to stay alive."*
> *Barbara Joe Williams*

APPENDIX 1
STANDARD BOOK PUBLISHING PROPOSAL

Dear Author,

Thank you very much for your interest in our services.

Vike Springs Publishing Ltd. is an international publishing house based in London, United Kingdom, and a proud member of **IBPA** (Independent Book Publishers Association) **USA**. As a Publishing House we are driven by the vision to work with authors in publishing world-class quality books and giving them maximum exposure around the globe. We are confident that with our team of industry professionals we can work with you to help you share your work, expertise, and knowledge with the global community.

Our **Comprehensive Self-Publishing** packages, we believe, would be of great benefit to you. From comprehensive editorial and proofreading services, custom interior layout and cover design, standout author branding packages to effective marketing and promotion packages, these services have been put together to afford you the flexibility to choose the one that meets your unique needs. You will also enjoy the freedom of choosing the sale price and earn 100% of your royalties received from all major bookseller platforms worldwide.

COMPREHENSIVE SELF-PUBLISHING PACKAGES

Standard Packages	Silver	Gold	Platinum
ISBN Assignment & UPC Barcode	✓	✓	✓
Books in Print Registration	✓	✓	✓
Editorial Assessment	✓	✓	✓
Content Editing, Copyediting & Plagiarism Checks	✓	✓	✓
Proofreading	✓	✓	✓
Custom Book Interior Layout Design	✓	✓	✓
Custom Book Cover Design with 3D copies	✓	✓	✓
E-Book Formatting & Publishing	✓	✓	✓
Barnes & Noble "Read Instantly"	✓	✓	✓
One-on-One Support & S Media Marketing Advice	✓	✓	✓
Amazon "Look Inside" and Google Preview	✓	✓	✓
Worldwide Book Distribution	✓	✓	✓
Paperback and Hardback Publishing	✓	✓	✓
FREE Complimentary Author Paperback Copies *	TBC	TBC	TBC
Author Brand Promo (Electronic Flyer & Posters)	—	✓	✓
Social Media Intro Promo Launch	—	✓	✓
Audiobook Production & Publishing			✓
Marketing & Promotion	—	—	✓

Reach out to us for our two-page publishing proposal for your consideration.

We also offer ghostwriting services, and developmental writing services. Each of these options provide a great opportunity to get all your ideas and thoughts set out profession- ally, in a way that can have the maximum impact on your intended audience.

An added benefit of our services is helping you publish your book on all global book platforms, such as, **Amazon global**, **Barnes and Noble**, **Ingram**, **Kindle**, **Smashwords, Draft2Digital, Apple iBooks**, **Gardners & Extended Retailer, Odilo, WHSmith (Kobo)**, **Scribd, Baker & Taylor, Tolino, OverDrive, Bibliotheca, Palace Marketplace, Vivlio, Borrowbox, Everand, Fable, Hoopla, public libraries,** with direct access to **Independent Bookstore buyers** in the **USA, North America** and **Europe**, and many more, in both eBook, paperback, hardback and audiobook formats, as well as providing world class quality book printing services, delivered on time to your chosen address.

Your book would also be made available on the global book inventory system, accessed by independent booksellers, libraries, and wholesale book buyers around the world. We would love to hear from you on how we can work with you to make your work avail- able to the wider global community. We hope you find your best fit package from our full range of packages for your consideration. If not, we would be more than glad to deliver a custom package that meets your requirements.

Hope to hear from you soon. Thank you.

APPENDIX 2

AUTHOR REVIEWS

"To all authors and potential authors, there's one publishing company you cannot afford to ignore. It's Vike Springs Publishing based in the United Kingdom. You will have absolutely nothing to complain about in terms of quality, they're on top in that regard. … In addition to quality, Vike Springs has many options that allow customers to make a satisfying choice(s) in terms of cost, delivery, time and marketing. I've always had value for money dealing with them because their flexibility allows me to negotiate to suit my financial strength." **Stephen Boseah,** Author of ***The Complete Life. Köln - Germany***

"The support that Vike Springs Publishing Ltd gave me was incredible. I was particularly impressed with the support they gave in the area of author branding and book promotion. I am not sure other publishing houses go to the extent of getting you radio interviews and giving you daily advice on author branding … They were exceptionally patient with me and were always ready to go that extra mile to ensure the editing, promotion and marketing was on cue." **Clement Kwegyir-Afful,** Author of ***Delivering Successful Megaprojects. KAPM Services Limited - UK***

"… As a new author, Vike walked me through the entire process from picking a title for the book, editing, cover design, production, marketing. Vike is detail-oriented, organized and always open to constructive feedback, making my journey and relationship both effortless and pleasant. I recommend Vike Spring Publishing for … publishing, distribution and marketing of your book(s). I am confident that they would take your work to new heights." **Minister Nana Bediako,** Author of ***What I Wish I knew Before My 20th Birthday, New Jersey - USA.***

"Being a first-time author, my biggest challenge and concern was how would I market this book … I can safely say that Vike Springs has worked very diligently to make sure the book kick starts off on the right platforms with their marketing skills. … I have been very satisfied with the persistence and dedication of Vike Springs for steering the marketing platform in such a professional manner. Thank you, Victor Kwegyir!" **Jenny Mohan,** Author of ***The King of Katunga. Accra - Ghana***

"I have published and printed two books with Vike Springs Publishing so far. … They work with you from inception through formatting, proof reading, printing and finally to delivery. I like the fact that they are open to suggestions and give a listening ear. They deliver on promise and on time, their work is excellent…." **Rev. Dr. Kwaku Sapon Darkwa**, Author of ***Guarding Your Joy and The Wonders Of Gratitude.*** **Adabraka - Ghana**

ENDNOTES

1   Kwegyir, V. *Business 365: Daily Inspiration for Creativity, Innovation and Business Success*. Vike Springs Publishing Ltd (23 July 2020)

2   Wordsrated. *Global Book Sales Statistics*. https://wordsrated.com/glob- al-book-sales-statistics/

3   Wordsrated. *Ibid.*

4   Ghostwriting Founder. *How Many Books are Published Each Year [2024 Statistics]* https://blog.ghostwritingfounder.com/how-many-books-are-published-each-year- 2024-statistics/

5   Wordsrated. *Ibid.*

6   Wordsrated. *Ibid.*

7   Toner Buzz. *Eye-Popping Book and Reading Statistics [2024]* https://www.tonerbuzz. com/blog/book-and-reading-statistics/

8   *Steady Writing and Marketing = Success*. https://www.allianceindependentauthors. org/wp-content/uploads/2024/03/The-Big-Indie-Author-Data-Drop-2024.pdf

9   Blurb Blog/Self Publishing/Book Trends to Look for in 2024 https://www.blurb. com/ blog/book-publishing-trends/

10   Ibis World. *Global Book Publishing Industry Outlook (2024-2029)* https://www.ibis-world.com/global/market-research-reports/global-book-publishing-industry/#IndustryStatisticsAndTrends

11   Future Market Insights/Book Publishers Market. https://www.futuremarketinsights. com/reports/book-publishers-market

12   International Publishing Association. *International Publishing Data 2023*. https:// internationalpublishers.org/international-publishing-data-2023/

www.ingramcontent.com/pod-product-compliance
Lightning Source LLC
Chambersburg PA
CBHW071112090426
42737CB00013B/2575